Written by: Pamela Amick Klawitter, EdD
Editor: Regina Kim
Designer/Production: Alicia Schulte
Cover Illustrator: Karl Edwards
Cover Designer: Barbara Peterson
Art Director: Moonhee Pak
Project Director: Stacey Faulkner

Table of Contents

Introduction

More I'm Through! What Can I Do? is a one-stop resource that addresses this all-too-familiar question teachers hear from students who finish early. The high-interest, ready-to-use puzzles, riddles, brainteasers, and mazes can be completed with minimal teacher assistance and help sharpen language arts, math, creative thinking, and critical thinking skills. This new series is a follow-up to our best-selling titles *I'm Through! What Can I Do?*

GETTING STARTED

Use any of the following suggestions to create a simple, structured environment that allows students to access these activities independently and keeps busy classrooms running smoothly.

1. Create individual student packets using all of the activity pages. Have students keep the packets in their desks and complete pages if they finish their assigned work early.

2. Create smaller packets by content areas (language arts and math) to use at centers. Store each set of packets in a file folder. Attach a class list to the outside of each folder. Have students cross out their names after they complete the packet.

3. Use activity pages individually as

- supplements to specific lessons
- homework assignments
- substitute teacher's helpers
- three-minute transition activities
- morning warm-up or after-lunch refocusing activities

HELPFUL TIPS TO FREE YOUR TIME

- Allow students to consult classmates to figure out puzzles.
- Encourage students to correct each other's work.
- Place copies of the answer key in an accessible area for students to pull as needed for self-correction.
- Give students copies of the Student Recording Sheet (page 4) to keep track of completed activity pages. Have students color in or check off each activity after it is completed.

However you choose to use the activity pages, let *More I'm Through! What Can I Do?* assist you in establishing a constructive and productive classroom environment.

Name: _____

Keep track of your work by filling in the box after completing the activity.

p. 5	p. 6	p. 7	p. 8	p. 9	p. 10	p. 11	p. 12	p. 13	p. 14
p. 15	p. 16	p. 17	p. 18	p. 19	p. 20	p. 21	p. 22	p. 23	p. 24
p. 25	p. 26	p. 27	p. 28	p. 29	p. 30	p. 31	p. 32	p. 33	p. 34
p. 35	p. 36	p. 37	p. 38	p. 39	p. 40	p. 41	p. 42	p. 43	p. 44
p. 45	p. 46	p. 47	p. 48	p. 49	p. 50	p. 51	p. 52	p. 53	p. 54
p. 55	p. 56	p. 57	p. 58	p. 59	p. 60	p. 61	p. 62	p. 63	p. 64
p. 65	p. 66	p. 67	p. 68	p. 69	p. 70	p. 71	p. 72	p. 73	p. 74
p. 75	p. 76	p. 77	p. 78	p. 79	p. 80	p. 81	p. 82	p. 83	p. 84
p. 85	p. 86	p. 87	p. 88	p. 89	p. 90				

Word Maker #1

How many words can you find in the Word Maker square? There are more than 50 words! Start your list below. Then challenge a friend to see who can find the most words.

Rules to remember:

- The words you find must have 3 or more letters.
- From any beginning letter, build a word by going left, right, up, down, or diagonally. (A single word may go in more than one direction.)
- You may not skip a square. Each letter in a word must touch the squares before and after it.
- The same letter square can be used more than once in a word, but it cannot be used twice in a row.
- The star can count for any letter, and it can be used twice in a row.
- Proper nouns (e.g., *John*) are not allowed.

l	e	m	t	s
r	a	o	n	i
o	p	★	c	d
b	a	r	d	e
w	e	l	i	t

_____   _____   _____

_____   _____   _____

_____   _____   _____

_____   _____   _____

_____   _____   _____

Word Maker #2

How many words can you find in the Word Maker square? There are more than 50 words! Start your list below. Then challenge a friend to see who can find the most words.

Rules to remember:

- The words you find must have 3 or more letters.
- From any beginning letter, build a word by going left, right, up, down, or diagonally. (A single word may go in more than one direction.)
- You may not skip a square. Each letter in a word must touch the squares before and after it.
- The same letter square can be used more than once in a word, but it cannot be used twice in a row.
- The star can count for any letter, and it can be used twice in a row.
- Proper nouns (e.g., *John*) are not allowed.

r	o	p	s	e
e	a	l	i	t
c	h	m	o	r
a	★	i	b	g
n	l	e	r	f

_____ _____ _____

_____ _____ _____

_____ _____ _____

_____ _____ _____

_____ _____ _____

More I'm Through! What Can I Do? Grade 6 © 2009 Creative Teaching Press

Word Maker #3

How many words can you find in the Word Maker square? There are more than 50 words! Start your list below. Then challenge a friend to see who can find the most words.

Rules to remember:

- The words you find must have 3 or more letters.
- From any beginning letter, build a word by going left, right, up, down, or diagonally. (A single word may go in more than one direction.)
- You may not skip a square. Each letter in a word must touch the squares before and after it.
- The same letter square can be used more than once in a word, but it cannot be used twice in a row.
- The star can count for any letter, and it can be used twice in a row.
- Proper nouns (e.g., *John*) are not allowed.

r	s	t	o	n
e	m	i	★	b
c	a	e	l	o
k	h	r	y	t
c	o	d	a	s

_____   _____   _____

_____   _____   _____

_____   _____   _____

_____   _____   _____

_____   _____   _____

More I'm Through! What Can I Do? Grade 6 © 2009 Creative Teaching Press

Word Maker #4

How many words can you find in the Word Maker square? There are more than 50 words! Start your list below. Then challenge a friend to see who can find the most words.

Rules to remember:

- The words you find must have 3 or more letters.
- From any beginning letter, build a word by going left, right, up, down, or diagonally. (A single word may go in more than one direction.)
- You may not skip a square. Each letter in a word must touch the squares before and after it.
- The same letter square can be used more than once in a word, but it cannot be used twice in a row.
- The star can count for any letter, and it can be used twice in a row.
- Proper nouns (e.g., *John*) are not allowed.

g	r	p	l	o
a	i	★	u	s
n	c	e	t	h
t	n	l	o	e
r	a	i	s	r

_____   _____   _____

_____   _____   _____

_____   _____   _____

_____   _____   _____

_____   _____   _____

More I'm Through! What Can I Do? Grade 6 © 2009 Creative Teaching Press

Name: _____   Date: _____

Four-Letter Frenzy

Arrange the letters into 24 four-letter words. Each letter may only be used once per word. No proper nouns!

Examples: moat, read

1. _____

2. _____

3. _____

4. _____

5. _____

6. _____

7. _____

8. _____

9. _____

10. _____

11. _____

12. _____

13. _____

14. _____

15. _____

16. _____

17. _____

18. _____

19. _____

20. _____

21. _____

22. _____

23. _____

24. _____

Dial-a-Letter

Make four-letter words by selecting a letter on each dial below. The letters must be used in the order of the spinners shown.

Example: meat

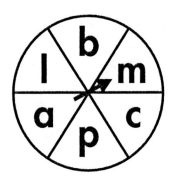   

1. _____

2. _____

3. _____

4. _____

5. _____

6. _____

7. _____

8. _____

9. _____

10. _____

11. _____

12. _____

13. _____

14. _____

15. _____

16. _____

17. _____

18. _____

19. _____

20. _____

More I'm Through! What Can I Do? Grade 6 © 2009 Creative Teaching Press

Monstrous Mix-up

Use the letters below to create words to fit in each column. A letter **may** be used more than one time in the same word. No proper nouns allowed.

L S A E R T H D

Example: 5-letter → start
6-letter → desert

5-Letter Words	6-Letter Words

From Start to Finish

Complete each word below by placing letters from the box between the starting and ending letters given. A letter may only be used once per word. No proper nouns.

Example: f __ __ __ t → frost, faint, first, feast

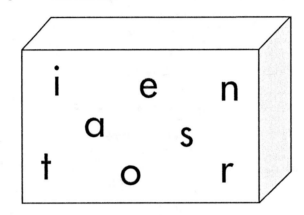

i   e   n
a   s
t   o   r

1. b __ __ __ s **and** b __ __ __ s

2. d __ __ __ y **and** d __ __ __ y

3. s __ __ __ e **and** s __ __ __ e

4. s __ __ __ s **and** s __ __ __ s

5. b __ __ __ n **and** b __ __ __ n

6. c __ __ __ e **and** c __ __ __ e

7. r __ __ __ s **and** r __ __ __ s

8. t __ __ __ t **and** t __ __ __ t

9. l __ __ __ r **and** l __ __ __ r

10. p __ __ __ t **and** p __ __ __ t

More I'm Through! What Can I Do? Grade 6 © 2009 Creative Teaching Press

Name: _____   Date: _____

Find the answer to the riddle by writing a letter for each picture symbol on the lines below. The first letter has been done for you.

A	B	C	D	E	F	G	H	I	J	K	L	M
●	◄	☯	□	★	☺	◉	&	☾	⌂	✺	➤	✓

N	O	P	Q	R	S	T	U	V	W	X	Y	Z
⚑	👍	💧	❀	☒	〰	♈	♓	◆	✦	❖	❁	➤

What do snakes do after they have a fight?

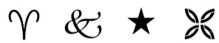

T _ _ _   _ _ _ _

_ _ _   _ _ _ _   _ _ .

More I'm Through! What Can I Do? Grade 6 © 2009 Creative Teaching Press

Code Breaker #2

Find the answer to the riddle by writing a letter for each picture symbol on the lines below. The first letter has been done for you.

A	B	C	D	E	F	G	H	I	J	K	L	M
●	◄	☯	□	★	☺	◉	&	☾	◫	☼	►	✓

N	O	P	Q	R	S	T	U	V	W	X	Y	Z
⚑	👍	💧	✿	⊠	≈	♈	♓	◆	✦	❖	❀	➤

Why was the baby ant always confused?

◄ ★ ☯ ● ♓ ≈ ★   ● ► ►

B _ _ _ _ _ _ _   _ _ _

& ☾ ≈   ♓ ⚑ ☯ ► ★ ≈

_ _ _   _ _ _ _ _ _

✦ ★ ⊠ ★   ● ⚑ ♈ ≈

_ _ _ _   _ _ _ _ .

Name: _____   Date: _____

Code Breaker #3

Find the answer to the riddle by writing a letter for each picture symbol on the lines below. The first letter has been done for you.

A	B	C	D	E	F	G	H	I	J	K	L	M
●	◄	☯	□	★	☺	◉	&	☾	⌂	☼	►	✔

N	O	P	Q	R	S	T	U	V	W	X	Y	Z
⚑	👍	💧	❀	☒	♒	♈	♓	◆	✦	❖	✤	➤

What can you sit on, sleep on, and brush your teeth with?

●   ☯ &   ●   ☾   ☒   ●

A __ __ __ __ __ __ , __

◄   ★   □   ●   ⚑   □   ●

__ __ __ , __ __ __ __

♈ 👍 👍 ♈ & ◄ ☒ ♓ ♒ &

__ __ __ __ __ __ __ __ __ __ !

Underwater Exploration

How many words can you make using the letters in **underwater exploration**? Start your list on the lines below. Challenge a friend to beat your score!

Rules to remember:

- Each word must have at least three letters.
- Use only the letters you see in **underwater exploration**.
- You may only use a letter as many times as it appears. For example, you may not have a word with two **i**'s because there is only one **i** in **underwater exploration**.
- No proper nouns (e.g., *John*).

Scoring:

Three-letter word	= 1 point
Four-letter word	= 2 points
Five-letter word	= 3 points
Six or more letters	= 4 points

_____   _____   _____

_____   _____   _____

_____   _____   _____

_____   _____   _____

_____   _____   _____

_____   _____   _____

_____   _____   _____

_____   _____   _____

_____   _____   _____

_____   _____   _____

_____   _____   _____

_____   _____   _____

More I'm Through! What Can I Do? Grade 6 © 2009 Creative Teaching Press

Surfing Adventure

How many words can you make using the letters in **surfing adventure**? Start your list on the lines below. Challenge a friend to beat your score!

Rules to remember:

- Each word must have at least 3 letters.
- Use only the letters you see in **surfing adventure**.
- You may only use a letter as many times as it appears. For example, you may not have a word with two **a**'s because there is only one **a** in **surfing adventure**.
- No proper nouns (e.g., *John*).

Scoring:

Three-letter word	= 1 point
Four-letter word	= 2 points
Five-letter word	= 3 points
Six or more letters	= 4 points

_____   _____   _____
_____   _____   _____
_____   _____   _____
_____   _____   _____
_____   _____   _____
_____   _____   _____
_____   _____   _____
_____   _____   _____
_____   _____   _____
_____   _____   _____
_____   _____   _____
_____   _____   _____

More I'm Through! What Can I Do? Grade 6 © 2009 Creative Teaching Press

Name: _____   Date: _____

Measure Up Crossword

Read each clue and figure out the answer. Write the number word in the grid below.

Across

1. Number of pints in eleven quarts.
4. Number of inches in a foot and a half.
6. Three more than two dozen.
9. Number of ounces in three pounds.
10. Number of quarters in seven dollars.
11. Number of quarts in six gallons.
12. Number of feet in twenty-two yards.

Down

2. Number of days in twelve weeks.
3. Number of nickels in $1.25.
5. Number of months in six years.
7. Number of hours in a day and a half.
8. Number of weeks in a year.

More I'm Through! What Can I Do? Grade 6 © 2009 Creative Teaching Press

Name: _____   Date: _____

State Scrambler Crossword

Unscramble the state names below. Write the correctly spelled words in the puzzle grid. You may need to look at a U.S. map.

Across

3. LARDMANY
5. FOILCANAIR
8. MYWIGON
9. TONHR AROCINLA
11. LOOKAHAM
12. BANKEARS

Down

1. WAGONTHINS
2. ISNOTMEAN
4. WADEREAL
6. IANANDI
7. TEENSENSE
10. SARASANK

Name: _____   Date: _____

Endangered Animals Word Search

Circle each endangered animal word in the grid below. Words may run up, down, left, right, or diagonally. Check the word off the list when you find it.

- ❏ American alligator
- ❏ Atlantic salmon
- ❏ Bactrian camel
- ❏ bald eagle
- ❏ black rhinoceros
- ❏ blue whale
- ❏ California condor
- ❏ cheetah
- ❏ Florida panther
- ❏ giant panda
- ❏ gray whale
- ❏ gray wolf
- ❏ grizzly bear
- ❏ mountain gorilla
- ❏ orangutan
- ❏ sea otter
- ❏ Siberian tiger
- ❏ snow leopard
- ❏ spotted owl
- ❏ Sumatran tiger
- ❏ whooping crane

```
C F L O R I D L E M A C N A I R T C A B
A Z N W R E S A L M S I B E R A S R P A
L Z L H P A L L I R O G N I A T N U O M
I I U O B A C T R F U O L E M S N O W R
F L E O U I C T A O N J O H E N K L A E
O Y I P A B B E S R A S M R R N L T W H
R E G I T N A R T A M U S A I Y W E I T
N S R N L U L A I N A P I E C S O R T N
I H A G A I D D O G M I B B A N D A H A
A A Y C N C E O L U E N E Y N O E N A P
C O W R T A A L E T L S R L A W T D T A
O R H A I V G R A A A A I Z L L T T E D
N N A N C O L P K N S U A Z L E O S E I
D S L E S L E H C I Z Z N I I O P A H R
O T E A A C O A A M D W T R G P S R C O
R M A B L U E W H A L E I G A A E A N L
W I Z S M A M R G A R E G T T R L H A F
E H F L O W Y A R G Z A E D O D E M D S
N G I A N T P A N D A R R A R N I A R K
T B A C K S O R E C O N I H R K C A L B
```

More I'm Through! What Can I Do? Grade 6 © 2009 Creative Teaching Press

Extreme Sports Word Search

Circle each sport word in the grid below. Words may run up, down, left, right, or diagonally. Check the word off the list when you find it.

- ☐ ballooning
- ☐ BASE jumping
- ☐ BMX
- ☐ boardsailing
- ☐ bungee jumping
- ☐ caving
- ☐ hang gliding

- ☐ inline skating
- ☐ jet skiing
- ☐ motocross
- ☐ mountain biking
- ☐ rock climbing
- ☐ scuba diving
- ☐ skateboarding

- ☐ skydiving
- ☐ snorkeling
- ☐ snowboarding
- ☐ snowshoeing
- ☐ surfing
- ☐ wakeboarding
- ☐ whitewater rafting

```
J  S  Y  B  A  R  D  A  O  W  N  G  N  I  V  I  D  Y  K  S
E  E  B  A  S  H  R  C  T  H  B  I  K  I  K  N  G  A  N  K
A  M  T  S  C  U  B  A  D  I  V  I  N  G  B  A  O  O  D  A
D  O  X  S  O  U  N  V  Y  T  S  K  A  T  R  L  R  A  O  B
E  U  M  B  K  H  A  I  M  E  O  U  N  Y  M  K  O  T  N  U
V  N  C  X  B  I  N  N  O  W  S  S  A  E  E  I  C  C  A  N
I  T  O  G  A  M  I  G  R  A  A  I  L  L  M  D  K  W  G  G
N  A  G  N  S  R  X  N  O  T  I  R  I  O  I  E  C  A  O  E
G  I  N  I  E  O  G  I  G  E  L  N  E  V  N  K  L  I  T  E
N  N  I  D  J  C  G  D  R  R  G  T  B  I  G  A  I  D  T  J
I  B  T  R  U  B  L  R  I  R  I  E  E  D  R  S  M  R  B  U
D  I  A  A  M  O  I  A  S  A  N  R  I  A  U  Y  B  O  A  M
I  K  K  O  P  A  D  O  S  F  T  G  N  R  T  A  I  L  L  P
L  I  S  B  I  R  O  B  C  T  R  N  F  F  R  K  N  F  L  I
G  N  E  W  N  T  Y  E  A  I  D  I  H  U  E  I  G  N  O  N
G  G  N  O  G  G  X  T  R  N  N  O  J  N  S  N  G  I  O  G
N  B  I  N  L  K  Y  A  E  G  N  I  E  O  H  S  W  O  N  S
A  X  L  S  I  W  A  K  E  B  O  A  R  D  I  N  G  T  I  Z
H  O  N  B  A  K  S  S  O  R  C  O  T  O  M  A  B  R  N  A
A  R  I  B  O  A  R  D  S  A  I  L  I  N  G  L  O  O  G  X
```

More I'm Through! What Can I Do? Grade 6 © 2009 Creative Teaching Press

Name: _____ Date: _____

Word Chain #1

How long can you make each word chain? Continue each chain until you can't add another word. Look at the example, and follow the rules below.

Rules to remember:

- Begin with the words shown in each box.
- Follow the rule shown in the box.
- Add as many words as possible.
- You may not use a word more than once.
- No proper nouns (e.g., *John*).

Example: Each word in the chain must have 2 letters and begin with the last letter of the previous word. ⟶ *oh, hi, it, to, on, no, or*

---

1. Each word in the chain must have 4 letters and begin with the last letter of the previous word.

   ⟶ **face, even,**_____

   _____

   _____

---

2. Each word in the chain must have one more letter than the previous word and begin with the same letter each time. ⟶ **so, sad,**_____

   _____

   _____

---

3. Each word in the chain must begin with the last two letters of the previous word. ⟶ **moth,**

   these, _____

   _____

   _____

More I'm Through! What Can I Do? Grade 6 © 2009 Creative Teaching Press

Word Chain #2

How long can you make each word chain? Continue each chain until you can't add another word. Look at the example, and follow the rules below.

Rules to remember:

- Begin with the words shown in each box.
- Follow the rule shown in the box.
- Add as many words as possible.
- You may not use a word more than once.
- No proper nouns (e.g., *John*).

Example: Each word in the chain must have two letters and begin with the last letter of the previous word. ➔ *oh, hi, it, to, on, no, or*

1. Each word in the chain must begin with the same 2 letters as the previous word and must have 5

   letters. ➔ **stool, sting,** _____

   _____

   _____

2. Each word in the chain must have 5 letters and begin with the last letter of the previous word.

   ➔ **floor, route,** _____

   _____

   _____

3. Each word in the chain must begin with the same two letters as the previous word and have one

   less letter. ➔ **Tallahassee, tablecloth,** _____

   _____

   _____

More I'm Through! What Can I Do? Grade 6 © 2009 Creative Teaching Press

Addition Pathways

Begin with the "start" number. Move vertically or horizontally through the maze, one square at a time. Use addition to reach the "finish" number at the end of the path. Draw a line to show your path. No square may be used more than once, and some squares won't be used at all. You must end with the total in the "finish" box.

START 1	9	8	7	13	10	
	14	12	21	6	8	
	7	19	2	18	16	
	22	1	20	12	11	
	15	16	9	7	5	100 FINISH

START 12	7	34	21	5	21	
	13	10	2	16	28	
	34	29	35	29	33	
	15	9	31	26	40	
	39	19	22	1	12	199 FINISH

START 6	1	11	29	21	8	
	33	28	2	16	12	
	15	14	31	22	9	
	3	20	13	5	35	
	19	26	7	38	34	166 FINISH

More I'm Through! What Can I Do? Grade 6 © 2009 Creative Teaching Press

Subtraction Pathways

Begin with the "start" number. Move vertically or horizontally through the maze, one square at a time. Use subtraction to reach the "finish" number at the end of the path. Draw a line to show your path. No square may be used more than once, and some squares won't be used at all. You must end with the total in the "finish" box.

START 100	9	10	5	18	26	
	12	8	20	3	22	
	6	16	7	4	23	
	10	1	14	11	15	
	13	21	2	25	17	1 FINISH

START 200	19	12	31	9	10	
	13	20	9	14	8	
	16	11	15	27	17	
	33	29	31	18	25	
	21	26	30	22	28	20 FINISH

START 300	41	20	11	17	53	
	28	29	9	49	44	
	13	27	19	26	30	
	38	18	22	35	62	
	33	42	51	39	55	33 FINISH

Add On

Begin each problem at the ★ square. Follow the directions and write down the number where you land. At the end of each pair of directions, add and write the sum on the line. The first number is shown.

600		695				976		699
	666			599			888	
555	187		666		709			487
	545	589		650		906		577
799		800		★	119		444	
	180		775		599			600
		199		556		175		609
188	607				615			898
		654		105			695	

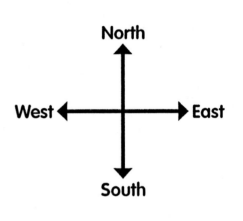

North

West ← → **East**

South

(1) N4, E4, S3 = ___**577**___

S3, E1, N3 = _____

Sum ➡ _____

(2) N3, W4, S1 = _____

W4, S2, E2 = _____

Sum ➡ _____

(3) N2, S6, N2 = _____

E2, S3, W5 = _____

Sum ➡ _____

(4) S1, E2, N5 = _____

N3, E3, S3 = _____

Sum ➡ _____

(5) S1, E2, N2 = _____

W4, S1, E5 = _____

Sum ➡ _____

(6) N2, W1, S3 = _____

S2, E4, N3 = _____

Sum ➡ _____

(7) S3, W2, S1 = _____

E4, N1, W6 = _____

Sum ➡ _____

(8) N3, W2, N1 = _____

W4, S2, E2 = _____

Sum ➡ _____

More I'm Through! What Can I Do? Grade 6 © 2009 Creative Teaching Press

What's the Difference?

Begin each problem at the ★ square. Follow the directions and write down the number where you land. At the end of each pair of directions, subtract and write the difference on the line. The first number is shown.

2101		2055		8091		7165		1342
	8210	1908	7765	4323	1097	2685	3633	
789	1000	2618	665	4166	2934	596	1032	2967
	7891	2001	8996	6012	9011	2987	2900	
6312	5046	1013	3299	1021	2109	7118	2702	2197
	7815	5005	3109	9064	3153	2071	2976	
6557	2198	3109	7381	2710	8091	1298	1079	3091
	7777	8003	1100	3769	1234	3071	6115	
9011		2205		★		6166		1919

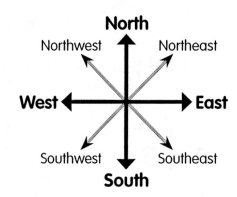

(1) NW3, NE2, W1 = **2001**

N8, SW4, E2 = _____

Difference ➞ _____

(2) NE4, NW1, S1 = _____

NW4, E8, NW3 = _____

Difference ➞ _____

(3) NE3, W4, SW3 = _____

N5, SW2, E1 = _____

Difference ➞ _____

(4) NE3, N4, W4 = _____

NW1, NE3, SE2 = _____

Difference ➞ _____

(5) NE1, NW3, S3 = _____

N4, NE1, NW3 = _____

Difference ➞ _____

(6) NW3, E3, SE2 = _____

N4, W1, SW2 = _____

Difference ➞ _____

(7) NW3, E4, S1 = _____

NE4, W5, N2 = _____

Difference ➞ _____

(8) N6, SE3, W3 = _____

NW4, NE3, SE1 = _____

Difference ➞ _____

Multiplication Mysteries

Begin each problem at the ★ square. Follow the directions and write down the number where you land. At the end of each pair of directions, multiply and write the product on the line. The first number is shown.

333		355		78		500		836	
64	321	75	726	355	363	369	399	595	656	682
	313	399	37	793	222	255	28	263	297
363	955	557	699	95	★	333	777	893	399	537
	897	13	279	353	630	387	703	27	45
56	756	860	159	389	883	599	38	853	357	378
	567		392		339		386		673

North
West ← → East
South

(1) N2, E3, S2 = **893**

   W3, S2, E5 = _____

   Product → _____

(2) S2, E3, N4 = _____

   W3, N2, W2 = _____

   Product → _____

(3) W4, N2, E2 = _____

   N2, W3, S3 = _____

   Product → _____

(4) E2, N2, W3 = _____

   S2, E2, N3 = _____

   Product → _____

(5) W3, S2, E2 = _____

   N1, E3, S2 = _____

   Product → _____

(6) W2, S2, E2 = _____

   S1, W3, N3 = _____

   Product → _____

(7) E3, N2, W3 = _____

   E2, S2, W7 = _____

   Product → _____

(8) N2, W2, S2 = _____

   S2, E4, N1 = _____

   Product → _____

More I'm Through! What Can I Do? Grade 6 © 2009 Creative Teaching Press

Division Dilemma

Begin each problem at the ★ square. Follow the directions and write down the number where you land. At the end of each pair of directions, divide the first number by the second and write the quotient on the line. Also write the remainder if there is one. The first number is shown.

27		675			487		36
	746		32			907	
555	43		699		755			600
	891	29		12		906		46
988		80		★	199		33	
	180		878		359			16
		199		556		778		71
188	895				48			898
		564		305			696	

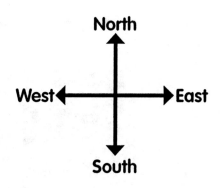

North

West ←→ East

South

(1) N4, E4, S2 = __**600**__

    S3, E3, N3 = _____

    Quotient → _____

(2) N3, W4, S1 = _____

    W4, S2, E8 = _____

    Quotient → _____

(3) N2, S6, N2 = _____

    E2, S3, W1 = _____

    Quotient → _____

(4) S1, E2, N5 = _____

    N3, E4, S2 = _____

    Quotient → _____

(5) S1, E2, N2 = _____

    W4, N1, E4 = _____

    Quotient → _____

(6) N2, W1, S3 = _____

    S2, E4, N3 = _____

    Quotient → _____

(7) S3, W2, S1 = _____

    E4, N1, W6 = _____

    Quotient → _____

(8) N3, W2, N1 = _____

    W4, N2, E1 = _____

    Quotient → _____

Math Path #1

Begin with the number next to the "start" box. Continue through the maze by adding, subtracting, multiplying, and dividing until you come to the "end." Write your final answer in the circle.

Start	861	+	269	÷
				5
				×
1,289	+	4	÷	8
−				
199				
×	7	+	999	◯ End

More I'm Through! What Can I Do? Grade 6 © 2009 Creative Teaching Press

Math Path #2

Start with the "input" number for each problem. Decide if the number is prime or composite. Follow the appropriate arrows below, and use the key to determine which operation to use to help you reach the output number.

Example: Input = 12. Since 12 is composite, complete the following steps to get an answer:

Input	= 12 (12 is composite)
12 x 48	= 576
576 + 599	= 1,175
1,175 – 666	= 509
509 x 38	= 19,342
Output	= 19,342

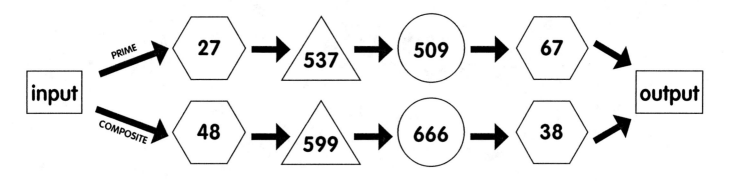

	Input	Output	Key
1.	17		⬡ = multiply
2.	21		
3.	23		△ = add
4.	35		
5.	37		◯ = subtract

Name: _____   Date: _____

Number Puzzle #1

Use the numbers and shapes in the Venn diagram below to answer each question.

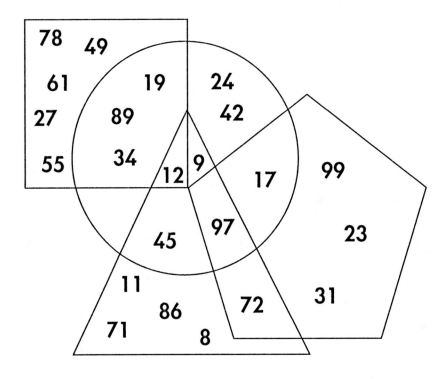

1. What is the sum of the numbers that are inside the circle but not inside the pentagon? _____

2. What is the product of the two largest numbers that lie anywhere inside the triangle? _____

3. What is the product of the two largest numbers that lie outside the circle? _____

4. What is the difference between the sum of **all** the numbers that lie inside the triangle and **all** the numbers that lie inside the pentagon? _____

5. Which shape has the largest sum when all numbers inside its border are added? _____

   What is the sum? _____

6. What is the product of the largest even number in the square and the largest odd number in the pentagon? _____

More I'm Through! What Can I Do? Grade 6 © 2009 Creative Teaching Press

Number Puzzle #2

Each piece of candy in the rectangle contains chocolate. Each piece in the circle contains raisins. Each piece in the triangle contains peanuts. Use this information to answer the following questions.

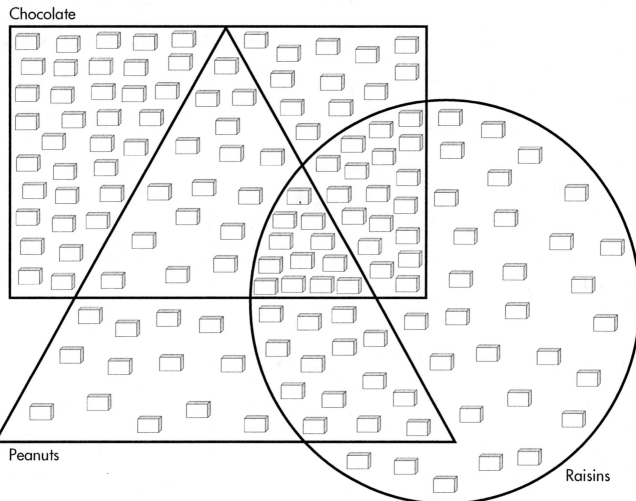

How many pieces of candy have...

1. only chocolate? _____

2. only raisins? _____

3. only peanuts? _____

4. raisins and chocolate, but no peanuts? _____

5. raisins and peanuts, but no chocolate? _____

6. chocolate and peanuts, but no raisins? _____

7. raisins, peanuts, and chocolate? _____

8. no chocolate? _____

9. no raisins? _____

10. no peanuts? _____

It All Adds Up #1

In this puzzle, there are 9 rows, 9 columns, and 9 mini-grids of 9 squares each. Using only the numbers 1 through 9, fill in the grid so that every row, every column, and every mini-grid of 9 squares contains the numbers 1 through 9. No number may be repeated within a column, row, or mini-grid.

6			9	1		4		7
	4	7	5			8		
8	9	3			6			
7	3	8		9				6
		2	3	8	5	9		
9				6			4	8
			8			7	9	4
		4			9	2	1	
2		9		3	4			5

More I'm Through! What Can I Do? Grade 6 © 2009 Creative Teaching Press

Name: _____   Date: _____

It All Adds Up #2

In this puzzle, there are 9 rows, 9 columns, and 9 mini-grids of 9 squares each. Using only the numbers 1 through 9, fill in the grid so that every row, every column, and every mini-grid of 9 squares contains the numbers 1 through 9. No number may be repeated within a column, row, or mini-grid.

8	3		1	9				4
9	4		6	7				1
				2	4	9	5	
		6	9	1	8	3		
3				5				9
		1	4	3	7	5		
	1	3	5					
7				6	1		9	5
6				4	2		3	8

Name: _____   Date: _____

It All Adds Up #3

In this puzzle, there are 9 rows, 9 columns, and 9 mini-grids of 9 squares each. Using only the numbers 1 through 9, fill in the grid so that every row, every column, and every mini-grid of 9 squares contains the numbers 1 through 9. No number may be repeated within a column, row, or mini-grid.

			7				9	3
2	9		6		4	5		7
5	7				2		6	
4				6	5			8
3	1		9		8	7		2
		5	2			1	4	
	5	4		2		8		
	6	9	4		7	3		
			5	1				

More I'm Through! What Can I Do? Grade 6 © 2009 Creative Teaching Press

Name: _____   Date: _____

It All Adds Up #4

In this puzzle, there are 9 rows, 9 columns, and 9 mini-grids of 9 squares each. Using only the numbers 1 through 9, fill in the grid so that every row, every column, and every mini-grid of 9 squares contains the numbers 1 through 9. No number may be repeated within a column, row, or mini-grid.

		4			1			8
8	6		3			9	4	
		5	8				3	7
6	5	7			9	3		
	8	3			7		6	9
2			1			8		
		8	9				5	3
4	3	1				7	9	6
	9				4	1		

Name: _____   Date: _____

It All Adds Up #5

In this puzzle, there are 9 rows, 9 columns, and 9 mini-grids of 9 squares each. Using only the numbers 1 through 9, fill in the grid so that every row, every column, and every mini-grid of 9 squares contains the numbers 1 through 9. No number may be repeated within a column, row, or mini-grid.

			3	5			6	4
		6		4	9	5		2
5		3						
8			9			3		1
						6	8	9
					5	4		7
9	5		6		4			
3	6		1			2		5
	2	1				9	7	

More I'm Through! What Can I Do? Grade 6 © 2009 Creative Teaching Press

Name: _____   Date: _____

It All Adds Up #6

In this puzzle, there are 9 rows, 9 columns, and 9 mini-grids of 9 squares each. Using only the numbers 1 through 9, fill in the grid so that every row, every column, and every mini-grid of 9 squares contains the numbers 1 through 9. No number may be repeated within a column, row, or mini-grid.

		1			7		3	
		2	5	1	9	7		
	6		2			1		
			9		2			
9		4	6			3	8	
8	2			3			1	7
6	4			2			7	9
	1	9			6	8		3
					4			

It All Adds Up #7

In this puzzle, there are 9 rows, 9 columns, and 9 mini-grids of 9 squares each. Using only the numbers 1 through 9, fill in the grid so that every row, every column, and every mini-grid of 9 squares contains the numbers 1 through 9. No number may be repeated within a column, row, or mini-grid.

3		2		4		6		
			2		1			
8	4		6	7		5		
	1		5		8		2	
9	3	6		2	7	8	5	
				1		7		6
	5	7			2		6	8
						2		3
2		3		4		9		

More I'm Through! What Can I Do? Grade 6 © 2009 Creative Teaching Press

It All Adds Up #8

In this puzzle, there are 9 rows, 9 columns, and 9 mini-grids of 9 squares each. Using only the numbers 1 through 9, fill in the grid so that every row, every column, and every mini-grid of 9 squares contains the numbers 1 through 9. No number may be repeated within a column, row, or mini-grid.

5	6			2			8	7
	9	2				1	3	
	4			7		2	6	5
3							2	
		4		5				9
	3		8	1	4		5	
6	1				7			
	2	8	5	6			9	

Get in Gear

Choose digits from the gears below to make the numbers required for each question. A digit may only be used once per number (for example, you may make 642 but not 662 because there is only one 6 shown). Be sure to show the number sentence you make to get the answer for the problem.

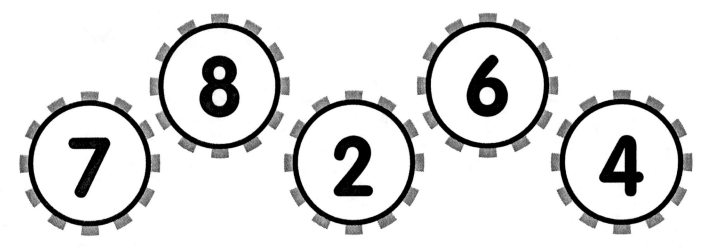

1. What is the difference between the largest and the smallest 4-digit numbers you can make? _____

2. What is the sum of the four largest 4-digit numbers you can make? _____

3. What is the difference between the largest even 5-digit number and the smallest odd 5-digit number you can make? _____

4. What is the sum of the five largest 3-digit numbers you can make? _____

5. What is the sum of the four largest 5-digit numbers you can make? _____

More I'm Through! What Can I Do? Grade 6 © 2009 Creative Teaching Press

Name: _____   Date: _____

Picking Apples

Choose digits from the apples below to make the numbers required for each question. A digit may only be used once per number (for example, you may make 938 but not 939 because there is only one 9 shown). Be sure to show the number sentence you make to get the answer for each problem.

1. What is the difference between the largest and the smallest 5-digit numbers you can make?

   _____

2. What is the sum of the five largest 3-digit numbers you can make?

   _____

3. What is the product of the two largest 3-digit numbers you can make?

   _____

4. What is the sum of the 10 smallest 2-digit numbers you can make?

   _____

5. What is the product of the largest 4-digit number and the smallest 2-digit number you can make?

   _____

Name: _____   Date: _____

B-I-N-G-O!

Use the *Bingo* card to answer the questions below.

	B	I	N	G	O	SUM
Row 1	15	17	44	59	68	____
Row 2	8	28	38	56	71	____
Row 3	13	22	FREE	49	75	____
Row 4	9	30	41	60	69	____
Row 5	12	19	35	48	73	____

SUM ____   ____   ____   ____   ____

Give the sum for each row and column on the lines provided above, and then answer the following questions.

1. Find the difference between the totals for the highest and lowest columns.   _____

2. How much more does the column **G** total than row **4**?   _____

3. Find the difference between the totals for the highest and lowest rows.   _____

4. What number would need to be removed from column **O** to make the total 285?   _____

More I'm Through! What Can I Do? Grade 6 © 2009 Creative Teaching Press

What's Missing?

Look at each series of words below. Figure out what the pattern is and add a word that continues the pattern. Then explain why your word is correct.

Example:

cot, den, elf, fit, _____ **gap** _____

Why? The next word must be a 3-letter word that begins with **g**.

1. apple, balls, crate, dance, _____

   Why? _____

2. Bill, Carl, Dave, Eddy, _____

   Why? _____

3. beef, deep, feet, heel, _____

   Why? _____

4. bomb, else, hatch, kick _____

   Why? _____

5. prove, order, nasty, mints, _____

   Why? _____

6. Ecuador, Denmark, Canada, Bolivia, _____

   Why? _____

7. October, prosper, quarter, rooster, _____

   Why? _____

8. Moe, mice, Maine, marine, _____

   Why? _____

Odd Word Out #1

In each row, all of the words have something in common except one. Find and circle the word that doesn't belong in each row.

1. nasty   malicious   compassionate   wicked   vicious

2. gigantic   massive   colossal   enormous   minute

3. wonderful   dreadful   superb   fantastic   fabulous

4. fictional   unreal   made up   factual   imaginary

5. fearful   frightened   afraid   scared   courageous

6. embark   finish   conclude   complete   cease

7. tooth   youth   mouth   truth   sleuth

8. Bolivia   Paraguay   Brazil   Libya   Ecuador

9. avocado   daffodil   marigold   geranium   daisy

10. blue   crimson   turquoise   aqua   sapphire

More I'm Through! What Can I Do? Grade 6 © 2009 Creative Teaching Press

Odd Word Out #2

In each row, all of the words have something in common except one. Find and circle the word that doesn't belong in each row.

1. Dallas	Tallahassee	Albany	Boston	Columbus
2. bellow	scream	screech	squeal	murmur
3. weird	unusual	ordinary	bizarre	curious
4. friend	niece	uncle	nephew	mother
5. Europe	Africa	Canada	Antarctica	Asia
6. acorn	apple	daisy	peach	coconut
7. Egypt	France	Sweden	Scotland	Spain
8. one	five	four	three	seven
9. joy	happiness	delight	pleasure	grief
10. flamingo	ostrich	swan	herring	goose

The Race Is Over

The winning car is pictured below. Which one is it? Use the clues to cross off one car at a time to figure out which is the winner.

1. The car's ID number has at least one odd digit on it.
2. The product of the first two digits on the car's ID number is more than 5.
3. The sum of the digits on the car's ID number is more than 10.
4. The difference between the first and last digit of the car's ID number is less than 5.
5. The car's ID number is not evenly divisible by 3.

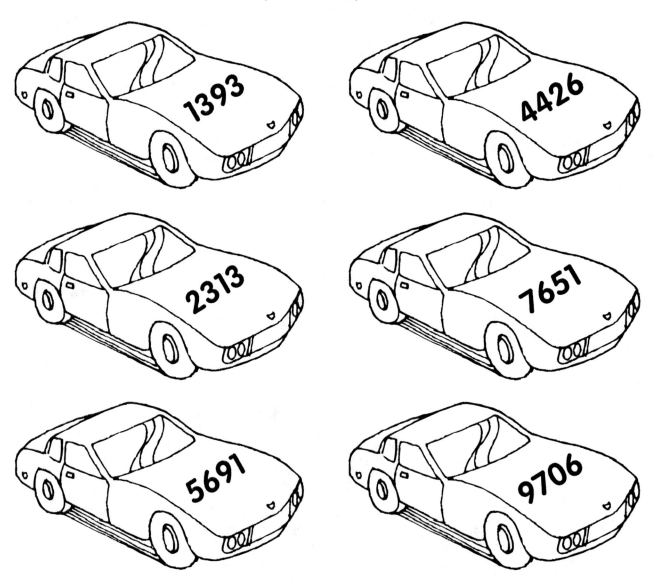

The winning car is # _____.

More I'm Through! What Can I Do? Grade 6 © 2009 Creative Teaching Press

Puppy Predicament

One of the ID tags below is for your new puppy, Darby. Use the clues to cross off one tag at a time to figure out which tag is Darby's.

1. The ID number on Darby's tag has at least one even digit.
2. The difference between the largest and smallest digits on Darby's tag is greater than 3.
3. The sum of the digits on Darby's tag is not 19.
4. The number on Darby's tag is greater than 65 x 75.
5. Darby's ID number is not equal to 878 x 8.

Darby's ID number is # _____.

Cabin Chaos

Your family arrived at the ski lodge to discover that all the cabins looked alike. Luckily each cabin has a number. Use the clues to cross off one cabin at a time until you figure out which one is yours.

1. Your family's cabin number is greater than 47 x 33.
2. The number is not equal to 2222 + 3957.
3. The cabin number is not evenly divisible by 2.
4. The sum of the first two digits is not equal to the sum of the second two digits on your cabin's number.
5. The number is not equal to 13542 ÷ 6.
6. The number is not equal to 5329 – 3452.

Your family's cabin number is #_____.

More I'm Through! What Can I Do? Grade 6 © 2009 Creative Teaching Press

Who's Who?

Help match each of the six new teachers' last names to the subject he teaches. Use the grid below to help you find out who's who.

Use the following rules:
- When a possible answer is false, place an X in the box.
- When you find a match, draw a black dot in the box.
- Once you place a dot for a subject, no one else can have that subject, so fill the rest of that subject's boxes with Xs.
- Once someone is matched with a subject, fill the rest of that person's boxes with Xs since he can't have more than one subject.
- When there is only one empty box remaining in a row or column of Xs, that must be the true answer, so place a black dot there.
- When you are finished, make sure there is one black dot for each name and each subject.

Use these clues **in order**. They will help you complete the chart below.
1. No teacher teaches a subject that begins with the same letter as his last name.
2. The subject Mr. Flagg teaches has more letters than his last name.
3. The subject Mr. Stewart teaches has fewer letters than his last name.
4. Mr. Hanover's subject has the same number of letters as his last name.
5. Mr. Mitchell's subject has the longest name.
6. The French teacher's last name has the fewest letters.
7. Mr. Eskell does not teach science.
8. The science teacher's last name has two of the same letter in it.

	Mitchell	Eskell	Gill	Stewart	Flagg	Hanover
Math						
English						
Geography						
Science						
French						
History						

Name: _____   Date: _____

State of Confusion

Each girl lives in a different state. Use the grid below to help you find out who lives where.

Use the following rules:
- When a possible answer is false, place an X in the box.
- When you find a match, draw a black dot in the box.
- Once you place a dot for a state, no one else can live in that state, so fill boxes with Xs under that state's name.
- Once someone is matched with a state, fill the rest of her boxes with Xs since someone can't live in more than one state.
- When there is only one empty box remaining in a row or column of Xs, that must be the true answer, so place a black dot there.
- When you are finished, make sure there is one black dot for each girl.

Use these clues **in order**. They will help you complete the chart below.
1. No girl's first name begins with the same letter as the state where she lives.
2. Neither Veronica nor Margaret lives in a state with a two-word name.
3. Allison's state has one more letter than her name.
4. The name of the girl who lives in Minnesota has four fewer letters than the state.
5. Kristin does not live in South Carolina.

	Kentucky	Minnesota	New York	Alabama	Vermont	South Carolina
Sarah						
Naomi						
Allison						
Kristin						
Veronica						
Margaret						

More I'm Through! What Can I Do? Grade 6 © 2009 Creative Teaching Press

Birthday Month Mix-up

These six boys were born in the same year, but each boy was born in a different month. Use the grid below to help you find out in which month each boy was born.

Use the following rules:
- When a possible answer is false, place an X in the box.
- When you find a match, draw a black dot in the box.
- Once you place a dot for a month, no one else can have that month, so fill boxes with Xs under that month.
- Once someone is matched with a month, fill the rest of his boxes with Xs since he can only have one birth month.
- When there is only one empty box remaining in a row or column of Xs, that must be the true answer, so place a black dot there.
- When you are finished, make sure there is one black dot for each boy.

Use these clues **in order**. They will help you complete the chart below.
1. No boy was born in a month that begins with the same letter as his name.
2. Mark was born latest in the year.
3. Only two of the boys were born earlier in the year than Jose.
4. Derek's name has more letters than the month in which he was born.
5. Fred wasn't born in January.
6. Adam was born before Max.

	January	February	March	April	May	December
Jose						
Mark						
Fred						
Derek						
Max						
Adam						

Name: _____   Date: _____

Token Logic #1

Cut out the 9 tokens. Use the clues below to help place the tokens in the correct squares on the grid. After reading all clues, you may have a token left over. Assume it fits in the last empty box. When you are finished, check to make sure all clues are still true!

Clues

- The ☾ tokens are on the left, but they do not touch.
- One of the ☯ tokens is between two ☾ tokens.
- The ⚲ token is in the center column, but does not touch either ☾ token.
- Only one ★ is in the bottom row, and it touches the other ★ token.
- The ☺ does not touch ☾ or ⚲.
- There is no ☯ on the bottom row.

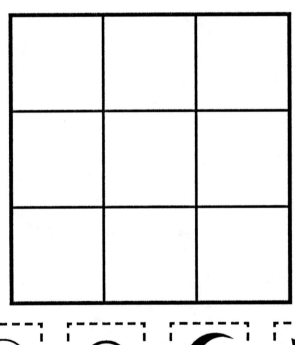

More I'm Through! What Can I Do? Grade 6 © 2009 Creative Teaching Press

Token Logic #2

Cut out the 9 tokens. Use the clues below to help place the tokens in the correct squares on the grid. After reading all clues, you may have a token left over. Assume it fits in the last empty box. When you are finished, check to make sure all clues are still true!

Clues

- The ☾ tokens are in the right-hand column, but they do not touch.
- Both ☺ tokens are in the center column, but neither is in the bottom row.
- The ▲ token is to the left of one of the ☺ tokens but not in the middle row.
- The ✺ token is in the middle column.
- The ● tokens are not in the same row, nor the same column.

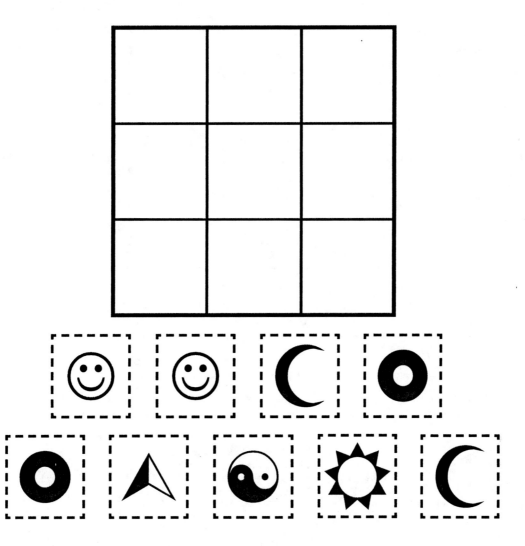

Token Logic #3

Cut out the 9 tokens. Use the clues below to help place the tokens in the correct squares on the grid. After reading all clues, you may have a token left over. Assume it fits in the last empty box. When you are finished, check to make sure all clues are still true!

Clues

- The ☯ tokens are in the bottom row, but they do not touch.
- The ★ token touches both the ☯ tokens.
- The ☺ is in the center.
- Neither of the ⋀ tokens are in the right-hand column, and they do not touch each other.
- The ⬤ are not in the same row and they do not touch each other.

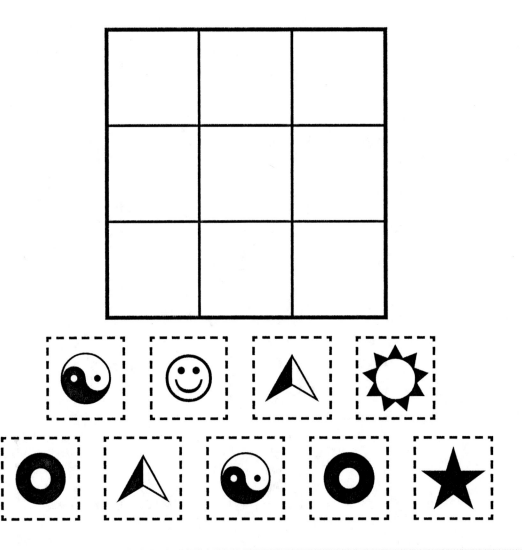

More I'm Through! What Can I Do? Grade 6 © 2009 Creative Teaching Press

Phone Tag

The keys below represent the keys on a typical phone. Refer to them as you complete the table below. For each line, use the letters on the specified number keys to make two words that each contain the required number of letters. A letter **may** be used more than once per word, but **no** proper nouns.

Example: 3-letter word using only the keys in the middle column ➡ *cat, jab, act, but, cub*

	# Letters	*Rule:* Use only the…	Two Words	
1.	3	…top row		
2.	3	…middle row		
3.	3	…bottom row		
4.	4	…left column		
5.	4	…middle column		
6.	4	…right column		
7.	4	…even-numbered keys		
8.	4	…odd-numbered keys		
9.	5	…even-numbered keys		
10.	5	…odd-numbered keys		
11.	6	…even-numbered keys		
12.	6	…odd-numbered keys		

Name: _____   Date: _____

Word$ Worth

Choose letters from the 1¢, 5¢, or 10¢ banks below to complete the words that follow each pattern shown. Come up with two words that follow each pattern. A letter **may** be used more than once. **No** proper nouns.

Example: ① ① ① ⑤ ➔ *rate, pain, craw, tire*

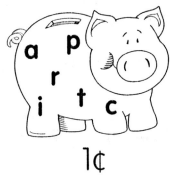

1¢

5¢

10¢

	# Letters	Word #1	Word #2
1.	① ① ① ①		
2.	⑤ ① ① ⑤		
3.	⑩ ⑩ ⑩ ①		
4.	⑩ ⑩ ⑤ ⑤		
5.	① ① ⑤ ⑤		
6.	⑤ ① ① ①		
7.	① ⑩ ⑩ ①		
8.	⑤ ⑤ ⑩ ①		
9.	⑩ ① ① ①		
10.	① ① ① ①		
11.	① ⑩ ① ⑩		

More I'm Through! What Can I Do? Grade 6 © 2009 Creative Teaching Press

Lucky Keystrokes

Come up with two words that follow each pattern given. A letter may **not** be used more than once per word. **No** proper nouns.

Example: M-M-M-T ➡ *fade, last, sage, halo*

T = Top ➡ **Q W E R T Y U I O P**

M = Middle ➡ **A S D F G H J K L**

B = Bottom ➡ **Z X C V B N M**

	Pattern	Word #1	Word #2
1.	M-T-M-B		
2.	M-M-M-T		
3.	B-M-M-T		
4.	T-T-M-M		
5.	B-T-M-M		
6.	B-M-M-M-T		
7.	B-M-M-T-T		
8.	T-T-T-T-M		
9.	T-T-M-B-T		
10.	T-M-T-T-T		
11.	M-M-T-T-T		
12.	T-T-B-M-M		

Name: _____   Date: _____

Put It All Together

Use the letters below to complete the words in the box. A letter **may** be used more than once in a word. **No** proper nouns.

Example: __ __ oo __ __ → *droops, brooms, shoots*

p   t   d   n   g   b
m   s   k   h
w   r   c

wrings

	Word #1	Word #2	Word #3
1.	__ __ in	__ __ in __	__ __ in __ __
2.	__ __ an	__ __ an __	__ __ an __ __
3.	__ ai __	__ __ ai __	__ __ ai __ __
4.	__ or __	__ __ or __	__ __ or __ __
5.	__ en __	__ en __ __	__ __ en __ __
6.	__ ee __	__ __ ee __	__ __ ee __ __
7.	__ ea __	__ __ ea __	__ __ ea __ __
8.	__ al __	__ __ al __	__ __ al __ __

More I'm Through! What Can I Do? Grade 6 © 2009 Creative Teaching Press

Name: _____ Date: _____

File It

Help! All the word files are mixed up! Build 4 words for each letter combination shown in the left–hand column—one word that would belong in each file drawer. The question marks may be replaced by one or more letters. Proper nouns may be used.

Example: ? ee ? → *deep, heed, proceed, street*

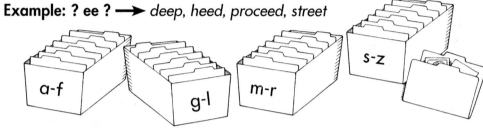

? ea ?	a-f		m-r	
	g-l		s-z	
? oo ?	a-f		m-r	
	g-l		s-z	
? ou ?	a-f		m-r	
	g-l		s-z	
? ai ?	a-f		m-r	
	g-l		s-z	
? at ?	a-f		m-r	
	g-l		s-z	
? or ?	a-f		m-r	
	g-l		s-z	
? er ?	a-f		m-r	
	g-l		s-z	
? st ?	a-f		m-r	
	g-l		s-z	

Name: _____ Date: _____

Color Pattern #1

Follow the directions below to complete this design:

1. Color all the factors of 240 *yellow*.
2. Color all the multiples of 13 *light blue*.
3. Color all the multiples of 7 *green*.
4. Color all the square numbers *red*.
5. Color all the prime numbers *light purple*.

Note: Spaces with no number remain white.

17	130	★ 23	65	47
48			80	
121	35	40	98	81
◇ 154	31	52 26 / 25 / 91 78	53	◇ 8
144	105	30	112	100
24			15	
29	117	★ 19	39	61

Color Pattern #2

Follow the directions below to complete this design:

1. Color all 1-syllable words **yellow**.
2. Color all 2-syllable words **light blue**.
3. Color all 3-syllable words **light green**.

4. Color all 4-syllable words **pink**.
5. Color all 5-syllable words **light purple**.

Note: Spaces with no number remain white.

hippopotamus	interior	cylinder	elevator	electricity
alligator	friend	baggage	splash	tarantula
arachnid	courage	carnivore	transit	elephant
registration	tracked	mirror	branch	photography
educational	inventory	calendar	category	deforestation

Satellite Radio

Use alphabetical order to help figure out which channel number has been assigned to each of the 12 new channels on the ZX Satellite Radio lineup. Write the number of each channel beneath its picture on the following page.

1. If *asteroid* comes before *astern* in the dictionary, write the number 108 for the "Classical" channel. If not, write a 104.

2. If *sturdy* comes after *stupendous*, write the number 100 for the "Seasonal" channel. If not, write a 102.

3. If *mandrake* comes before *mandolin*, write the number 105 for the "Sports" channel. If not, write a 109.

4. If *capacity* comes after *capability*, write the number 107 for the "Rock 'n' Roll" channel. If not, write a 103.

5. If *digital* comes after *dignified*, write the number 108 for the "Country" channel. If not, write a 101.

6. If *registration* comes before *registered*, write the number 111 for the "Jazz" channel. If not, write a 103.

7. If *villain* comes after *village*, write the number 105 for the "News 24/7" channel. If not, write a 106.

8. If *whirlpool* comes before *whirlybird* write the number 111 for the "Hip-Hop" channel. If not, write a 102.

9. If *appreciate* comes after *appreciation*, write the number 111 for the "All Talk" channel. If not, write a 106.

10. If *fidelity* comes before *fidgety*, write the number 102 for the "Latin" channel. If not, write a 110.

11. If *organize* comes after *organist*, write the number 108 for the "Bluegrass" channel. If not, write a 103.

12. If *imagination* comes before *imaginary*, write the number 105 for the "Oldies" channel. If not, write a 110.

More I'm Through! What Can I Do? Grade 6 © 2009 Creative Teaching Press

Satellite Radio

Jazz

Hip-Hop

Latin

Rock 'n' Roll

Seasonal

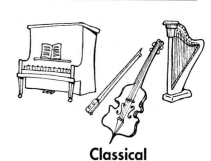

Classical

Country

Bluegrass

Oldies

All Talk

Sports

News 24/7

Get in Shape

Use the numbers and shapes in the Venn diagram to help answer each clue.

1. I am the largest number that lies inside both the circle and the square but in no other shape.   _____

2. I am the only number that lies inside the pentagon, the triangle, and the hexagon at the same time.   _____

3. I am the sum of all the numbers that lie inside the pentagon.   _____

4. I am the product of the two largest numbers inside the hexagon.   _____

5. I am the difference between the largest number inside the pentagon and the smallest number inside the triangle.   _____

6. I am the sum of the numbers that lie inside the circle but in no other shape.   _____

7. I am the sum of all the numbers that lie outside the pentagon.   _____

8. I am the only number inside both the triangle and the hexagon but in no other shapes.   _____

9. I am the sum of all the odd numbers inside the circle.   _____

10. I am the sum of all the numbers that lie in three different shapes at the same time.   _____

11. I am the product of the largest and smallest numbers inside the pentagon.   _____

12. I am the remainder when the largest number in the hexagon is divided by the smallest number in the circle.   _____

More I'm Through! What Can I Do? Grade 6 © 2009 Creative Teaching Press

Name: _____ Date: _____

Get in Shape

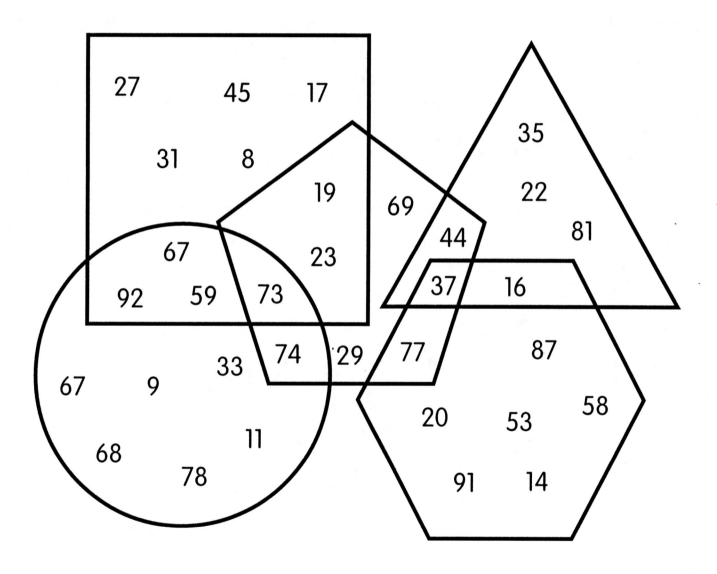

What's for Lunch?

Solve the math problems to help figure out which number belongs on each menu item. Write the correct number beneath each menu item on the following page.

1. If *483 + 279 = 782*, write the number 8 beneath the hot dog. If not, write a 10.

2. If *39 x 17 = 663*, write the number 4 beneath the spaghetti. If not, write a 5.

3. If *651 – 399 = 242*, write the number 7 beneath the salad. If not, write a 6.

4. If *769 + 376 = 1,045*, write the number 9 beneath the burger. If not, write a 12.

5. If *71 x 19 = 1,349*, write the number 5 beneath the ham and cheese sandwich. If not, write a 1.

6. If *2,403 ÷ 27 = 88*, write the number 6 beneath the fruit. If not, write a 9.

7. If *3,698 – 1,877 = 1,721*, write the number 2 beneath the soup. If not, write a 1.

8. If *966 + 594 = 1,560*, write a 7 beneath the "surprise" lunch bag. If not, write a 9.

9. If *1,211 – 888 = 333*, write a 10 beneath the taco. If not, write an 8.

10. If *286 x 12 = 3,432*, write a 3 beneath the macaroni and cheese. If not, write a 12.

11. If *795 + 869 = 1,564*, write an 11 beneath the Chinese food. If not, write a 2.

12. If *48 x 36 = 1,826*, write a 1 beneath the pizza. If not, write an 11.

More I'm Through! What Can I Do? Grade 6 © 2009 Creative Teaching Press

Name: _____   Date: _____

What's for Lunch?

Burger

Soup

Fruit

Salad

Spaghetti

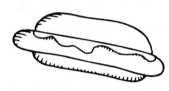

Hot Dog

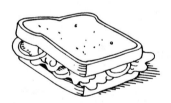

Ham and Cheese

Surprise

Taco

Chinese Food

Macaroni and Cheese

Pizza

Name: _____   Date: _____

Dazzling Design

Follow these directions to complete the "Dazzling Design" on the next page.

1. Draw a smiley face in the four corner boxes. Color the upper left-hand face yellow and the lower left-hand one blue. Color the lower right-hand face green. And the upper right-hand one red.

2. In the box just to the southeast of the yellow smiley face, draw and color a blue five-pointed star. In the box just north of the blue star, draw a big purple check mark.

3. Draw and color a big black X in the space three spaces to the right of the blue star and another one just north of the blue smiley face.

4. Just to the west of the green smiley face, draw a big blue check mark. Five spaces north of the blue check mark, draw and color a blue flower.

5. Between the purple checkmark and the blue flower, carefully print the current year with large black numbers. Five spaces directly south of the year, print your initials in big black letters.

6. Make two hearts, a red one just south of the date and a yellow one just north of your initials.

7. Finish the center column with two large diamonds. Color the top one purple and the bottom one black.

8. Draw and color an orange sun one space southwest of the purple check mark and a yellow sun one space northeast of the blue check mark. Finish the bottom row with a green flower.

9. In the third row, draw a red arrow pointing right in the left-hand box and a yellow arrow pointing west in the right-hand box. Just below the yellow arrow, draw a purple arrow pointing left. Just below the red arrow, draw a green arrow pointing right.

10. To the left and right of the yellow heart, draw a five-pointed star. Color the left one red and the right one black. Just north of the red star, draw a blue lightning bolt. North of the black star, draw and color an orange triangle.

11. Just west of the purple diamond, draw and color a green triangle. East of the purple diamond, draw an color a green lightning bolt.

12. In the remaining box, draw and color a yellow five-pointed star.

More I'm Through! What Can I Do? Grade 6 © 2009 Creative Teaching Press

Name: _____ Date: _____

Dazzling Design

Name: _____   Date: _____

Robot Design

Use colored pencils to color in the grid using these directions.

1. In rows 13, 14, 16, 17, and 19, color B, C, K, and L gray and boxes D through J green.

2. In row 1, color box G black; and in row 2, color boxes F, G, and H black.

3. In rows 4 and 9, color boxes E through I yellow.

4. In rows 25, 26, and 27, color boxes D, E, F, H, I, and J blue.

5. In rows 23 and 24, color boxes A, B, C, K, L, and M yellow and boxes D, E, F, H, I, and J blue.

6. In row 3, color boxes E through I black.

7. In rows 15 and 18, color boxes B, C, K, and L gray; boxes D, E, F, H, I, and J green; and box G brown.

8. In rows 29 and 30, color boxes B, C, D, E, F, H, I, J, K, and L black.

9. In rows 20 and 21, color boxes B, C, K, and L gray; boxes D, E, I, and J black; and boxes F, G, and H orange.

10. In row 5, color boxes E, G, and I yellow and boxes F and H blue.

11. In row 22, color boxes B, C, K, and L gray and boxes D, E, F, H, I, and J blue.

12. In row 11, color boxes C and K gray and boxes D through J green.

13. In row 6, color boxes D and J black; box G brown; and boxes E, F, H, and I yellow.

14. In row 12, color boxes B, C, K, and L gray; box G brown; and boxes D, E, F, H, I, and J green.

15. In row 10, color boxes F, G, and H yellow.

16. In row 8, color boxes E and I yellow and boxes F, G, and H red.

17. In row 7, color boxes D and J black and boxes E, F, G, H, and I yellow.

	A	B	C	D	E	F	G	H	I	J	K	L	M
1													
2													
3													
4													
5													
6													
7													
8													
9													
10													
11													
12													
13													
14													
15													
16													
17													
18													
19													
20													
21													
22													
23													
24													
25													
26													
27													
28													
29													
30													

More I'm Through! What Can I Do? Grade 6 © 2009 Creative Teaching Press

Draw a Police Pup

Follow these steps to draw Police Pup.

Draw the head and hat as shown.

Add the body.

Add details as shown.

Draw your finished Police Pup here.
Add background details and color.

Name: _____   Date: _____

Draw a Motorcycle

Follow these steps to draw a motorcycle.

1.

Draw the body as shown.

2.

Add the front fender and details as shown.

3.

Add the wheels.

4.

Draw the rest of the details.

Draw your finished motorcycle here. Add background details and color.

More I'm Through! What Can I Do? Grade 6 © 2009 Creative Teaching Press

Name: _____   Date: _____

Draw a Scene

Look at the scene below and copy it in the box at the bottom of the page.

Draw your finished scene here. Add background details and color.

Owl Portrait

Use the artwork on the left side of this page as a guide to help you complete the owl. Color your completed picture.

More I'm Through! What Can I Do? Grade 6 © 2009 Creative Teaching Press

Draw an Ostrich

Use the artwork on the left side of this page as a guide to help you complete the ostrich. Color your completed picture.

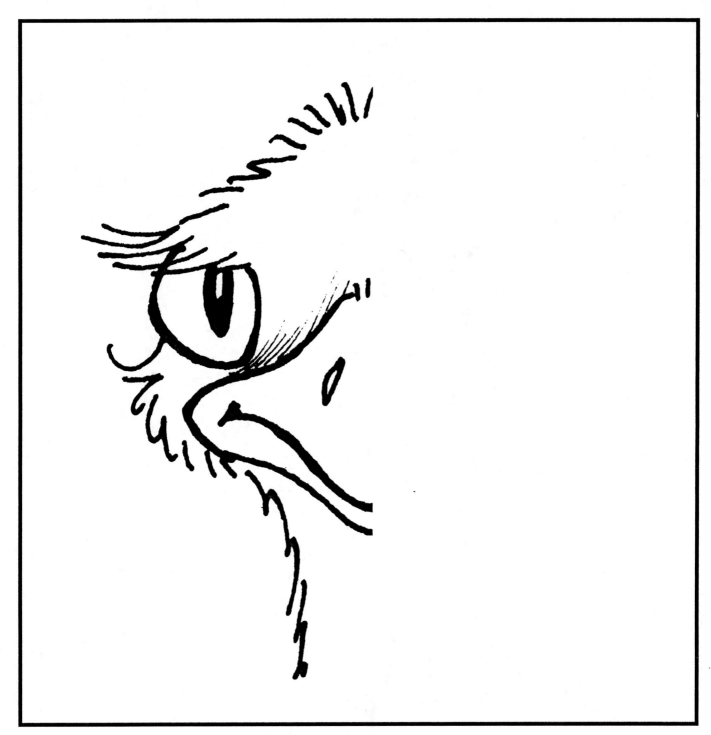

Create a Clown

Use the artwork on the left side of this page as a guide to help you complete the clown. Color your completed picture.

Name: _____   Date: _____

Design an MP3 Player Case

Design some cool cases for your MP3 player that feature your own original artwork. Draw the details and color them in.

Personal Banner

Design your own personal banner. Draw and color a picture, symbol, or slogan in each of the four sections to show four things that are important to you.

Name	Year

Design a CD Case

Design an original CD case for your favorite band or singer. Draw, color, and add fancy lettering.

Create Comic Strips #1

Create original comic strips. The central characters should be *animals*. Think of a funny situation for the characters, and draw one scene in each box below. Be creative!

Create Comic Strips #2

Create original comic strips. The central characters should be **people**. Think of a funny situation for the characters, and draw one scene in each box below. Be creative!

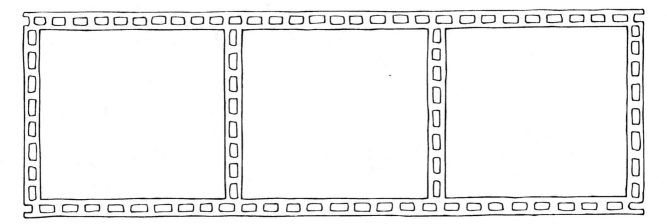

Grid Picture #1

Plot the ordered pairs in the order they are listed below. Connect the dots as you find each one. When you come to a ☆, start a new part of the picture without connecting it back to the dot before the ☆. Color your completed picture.

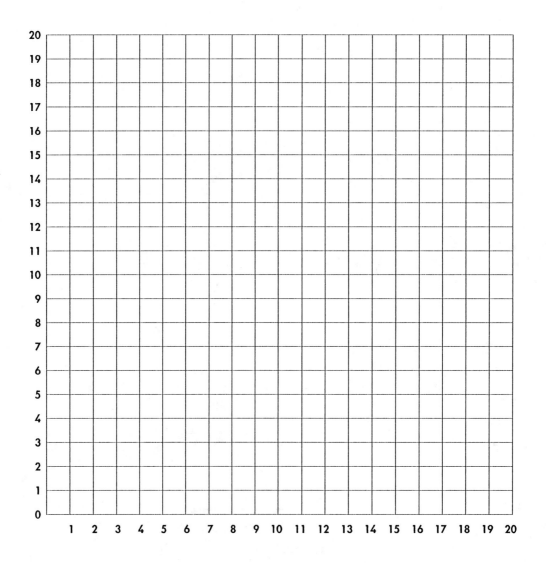

☆ (0, 6) (1, 5) (2, 6) (3, 5) (5, 6) (6, 5) (7, 6) (8, 5) (10, 6) (12, 5) (13, 6) (14, 5) (15, 6) (16, 5) (17, 6) (18, 5) (19, 6) (20, 5) ☆ (15, 9) (15, 8) (14, 8) (15, 9) ☆ (2, 6) (1, 7) (2, 10) (3, 12) (4, 13) (3, 14) (3, 16) (4, 15) (5, 14) (5, 13) (6, 15) (8, 16) (7, 14) (5, 12) (4, 10) (4, 9) (5, 8) (7, 9) (10, 11) (12, 12) (14, 12) (16, 10) (18, 8) (17, 7) (16, 5) ☆ (18, 8) (16, 7) (14, 7) (13, 8)

More I'm Through! What Can I Do? Grade 6 © 2009 Creative Teaching Press

Name: _____   Date: _____

Grid Picture #2

Plot the ordered pairs in the order they are listed below. Connect the dots as you find each one. When you come to a ☆, start a new part of the picture without connecting it back to the dot before the ☆. Color your completed picture.

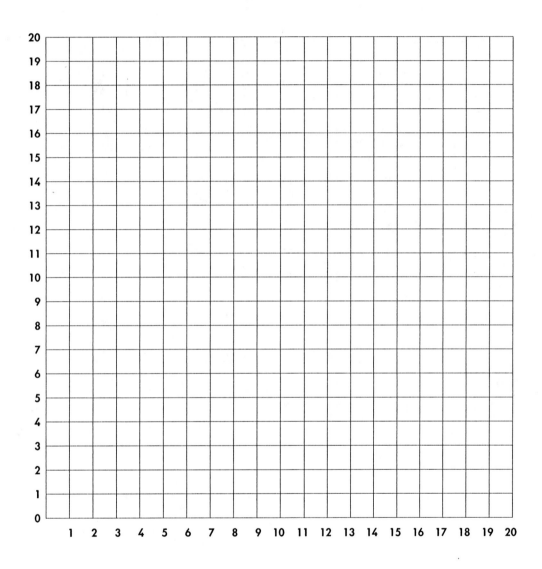

☆ (1, 10) (2, 12) (5, 13) (8, 13) (8, 15) (10, 17) (10, 15) (11, 13) (13, 12) (15, 15) (18, 17) (19, 17) (18, 15) (16, 12) (15, 11) (15, 10) (16, 9) (18, 6) (19, 4) (18, 4) (15, 6) (13, 9) (11, 8) (10, 7) (11, 4) (10, 5) (9, 3) (8, 7) (6, 7) (7, 6) (7, 4) (5, 7) (3, 8) (1, 10) ☆ (3, 8) (4, 8) (5, 9) ☆ (2, 10) (3, 11) (3, 10) (2, 10)

Grid Picture #3

Plot the ordered pairs in the order they are listed below. Connect the dots as you find each one. When you come to a ☆, start a new part of the picture without connecting it back to the dot before the ☆. Color your completed picture.

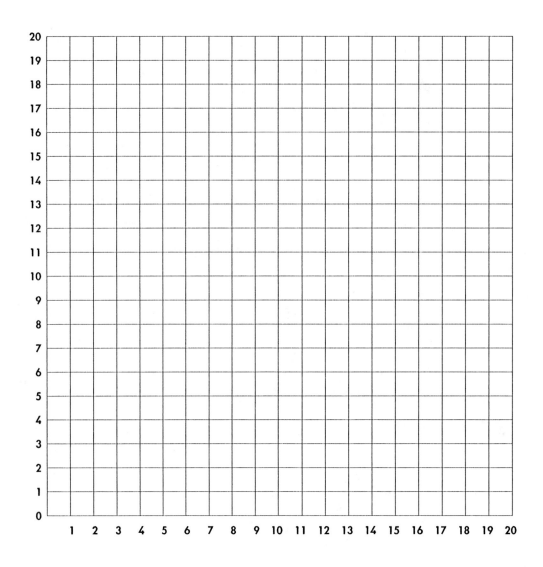

☆ (4, 0) (20, 0) (19, 7) (18, 8) (17, 6) (16, 7) (15, 6) (13, 5) (12, 6) (11, 4) (9, 5) (8, 4)
(8, 6) (7, 4) (5, 3) (4, 0) ☆ (19, 7) (20, 6) (20, 7) (19, 12) (17, 15) (16, 18) (13, 19) (8, 19)
(6, 18) (6, 17) (9, 14) (9, 12) (7, 11) (7, 9) (6, 7) (5, 5) (5, 3) ☆ (8, 9) (11, 12) ☆ (6, 17)
(2, 17) (0, 15) (0, 13) (2, 11) (2, 12) (3, 13) (7, 11) ☆ (3, 13) (6, 13) (8, 12)
☆ **shade in this shape →** (8, 16) (9, 17) (10, 16) (9, 15) (8, 16) ☆ (8, 17) (9, 18) (10, 17)

More I'm Through! What Can I Do? Grade 6 © 2009 Creative Teaching Press

Win the Race

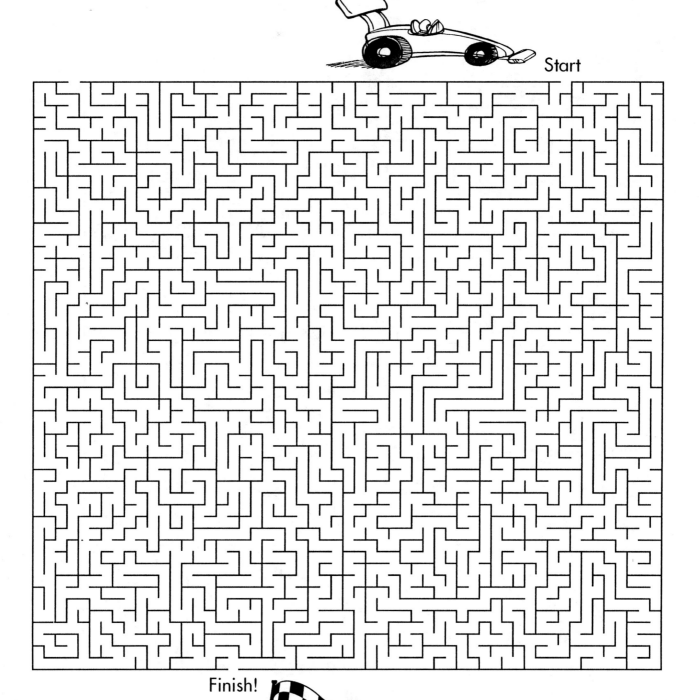

Start

Finish!

Sprint to the Finish Line

Start

Finish!

More I'm Through! What Can I Do? Grade 6 © 2009 Creative Teaching Press

Catch a Butterfly

Start

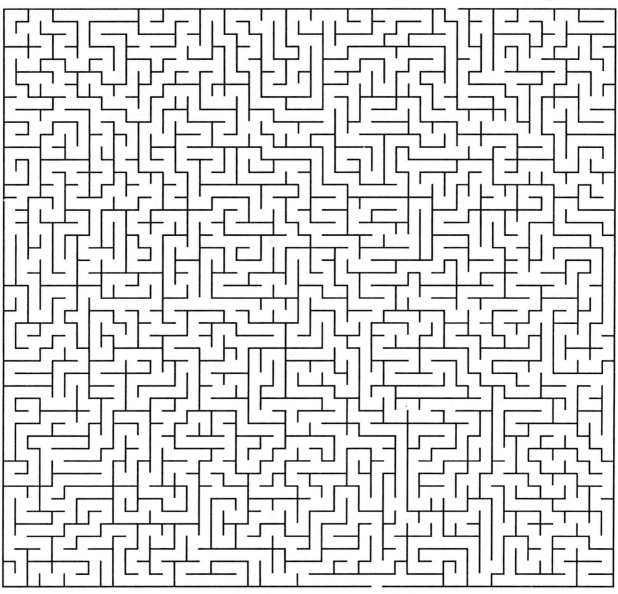

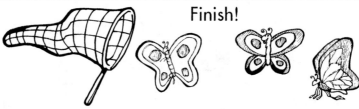

Finish!

Find the Way Home

Start

Finish!

More I'm Through! What Can I Do? Grade 6 © 2009 Creative Teaching Press

Answer Key

Word Maker #1 (Page 5)

Possible answers include:

apart	nomad
bard	once
barrel	pride
croons	prince
deduce	reason
diner	roam
into	snide
leap	stomp
meal	warped

Word Maker #2 (Page 6)

Possible answers include:

ache	nacho
calm	nail
chap	reach
either	ream
grips	roach
hale	roams
limit	split
mailer	tries
mites	trips

Word Maker #3 (Page 7)

Possible answers include:

bowler	noise
brim	notice
camera	opera
cares	otter
each	resist
emits	rest
hardy	robot
leer	timers
limes	trial

Word Maker #4 (Page 8)

Possible answers include:

blush	later
caret	luster
cent	picture
crisp	price
drain	pulse
grant	pushes
grip	rotten
hose	shuttle
ice	talent

Four-Letter Frenzy (Page 9)

Possible answers include:

1. dare	13. more
2. dart	14. rate
3. dime	15. road
4. dire	16. roam
5. dome	17. rode
6. dorm	18. tame
7. made	19. team
8. mart	20. time
9. mate	21. toad
10. meat	22. tore
11. mite	23. tram
12. mode	24. trim

Dial-a-Letter (Page 10)

Possible answers include:

1. ants	11. most
2. arts	12. mule
3. beds	13. must
4. boss	14. pads
5. busy	15. pear
6. colt	16. peel
7. cost	17. pest
8. less	18. pose
9. melt	19. prey
10. mole	20. puts

Monstrous Mix-up (Page 11)

Possible answers include:

5-Letter Words:

1. heart	7. steal
2. laser	8. tales
3. rates	9. tears
4. sales	10. there
5. stale	11. trade
6. stare	12. tread

6-Letter Words

1. dealer	7. stared
2. hearth	8. steals
3. leader	9. teased
4. rested	10. thread
5. slates	11. threat
6. sleets	12. traded

From Start to Finish (Page 12)

Possible answers include:

1. bears, bones, beats
2. dairy, dirty, daisy
3. snore, stare, snare

4. stirs, stars, seats
5. brain, bison, basin
6. crane, crate, canoe
7. rates, roses, rains
8. toast, trait, treat
9. liner, loser, later
10. point, print, paint

Code Breaker #1 (Page 13)

They hiss and make up.

Code Breaker #2 (Page 14)

Because all his uncles were ants.

Code Breaker #3 (Page 15)

A chair, a bed, and a toothbrush!

Underwater Exploration (Page 16)

Possible answers include:

3-Letter Words: not, pan, pit, ran, rat, rut, tar, tea, wad, wax

4-Letter Words: date, down, draw, pole, plow, rope, tint, wait, wear, wood

5-Letter Words: deter, drawn, expel, plane, pleat, polar, train, under, water, write

6 or More Letters: drawer, detour, duration, nation, national, plunder, ration, underwear, waiter, watered

Surfing Adventure (Page 17)

Possible answers include:

3-Letter Words: den, due, fig, fin, rat, rut, sad, sat, sin, sun

4-Letter Words: darn, dent, dive, dune, fang, gave, save, sing, surf, tree

5-Letter Words: darts, dents, fades, fangs, ruder, runts, sting, trade, turns, vents

6 or More Letters: avenue, dentures, endure, enduring, fading, friend, surfing, tending, trades, venture,

Measure Up Crossword (Page 18)

Across
1. twenty-two
4. eighteen
6. twenty-seven
9. forty-eight
10. twenty-eight
11. twenty-four
12. sixty-six

Down
2. eighty-four
3. twenty-five
5. seventy-two
7. thirty-six
8. fifty-two

State Scrambler Crossword (Page 19)

Across
3. Maryland
5. California
8. Wyoming
9. North Carolina
11. Oklahoma
12. Nebraska

Down
1. Washington
2. Minnesota
4. Delaware
6. Indiana
7. Tennessee
10. Arkansas

Endangered Animals Word Search (Page 20)

Extreme Sports Word Search (Page 21)

Word Chain #1 (Page 22)

Answers will vary.

Word Chain #2 (Page 23)

Answers will vary.

Addition Pathways (Page 24)

Top → $1 + 9 + 14 + 12 + 21 + 2 + 20 + 9 + 7 + 5 = 100$

Middle → $12 + 7 + 13 + 34 + 15 + 9 + 31 + 26 + 40 + 12 = 199$

Bottom → $6 + 1 + 11 + 29 + 21 + 8 + 12 + 9 + 35 + 34 = 166$

Subtraction Pathways (Page 25)

Top → $100 - 9 - 12 - 8 - 16 - 7 - 4 - 11 - 15 - 17 = 1$

Middle → $200 - 19 - 12 - 31 - 9 - 14 - 27 - 18 - 22 - 28 = 20$

Bottom → $300 - 41 - 20 - 11 - 9 - 19 - 22 - 51 - 39 - 55 = 33$

Add On (Page 26)

1. $577 + 119 = 696$
2. $555 + 199 = 754$
3. $556 + 607 = 1,163$
4. $976 + 444 = 1,420$
5. $906 + 599 = 1,505$
6. $775 + 577 = 1,352$
7. $654 + 589 = 1,243$
8. $695 + 199 = 894$

What's the Difference? (Page 27)

1. $2,001 - 1,013 = 988$
2. $2,702 - 1,097 = 1,605$
3. $9,011 - 3,109 = 5,902$
4. $7,765 - 3,091 = 4,674$
5. $8,003 - 2,055 = 5,948$
6. $3,071 - 2,198 = 873$
7. $8,091 - 665 = 7,426$
8. $9,064 - 4,166 = 4,898$

Multiplication Mysteries (Page 28)

1. $893 \times 38 = 33,934$
2. $595 \times 64 = 38,080$
3. $726 \times 13 = 9,438$
4. $355 \times 28 = 9,940$
5. $389 \times 27 = 10,503$
6. $883 \times 75 = 66,225$
7. $363 \times 56 = 20,328$
8. $699 \times 45 = 31,455$

Division Dilemma (Page 29)

1. $400 \div 33 = 12$ R4
2. $555 \div 71 = 7$ R58
3. $556 \div 48 = 11$ R28
4. $487 \div 46 = 10$ R27
5. $906 \div 12 = 75$ R6
6. $878 \div 46 = 19$ R4
7. $564 \div 29 = 19$ R13
8. $675 \div 43 = 15$ R30

Math Path #1 (Page 30)

End: 11,793

Math Path #2 (Page 31)

1. 32,629
2. 35,758
3. 43,483
4. 61,294
5. 68,809

Number Puzzle #1 (Page 32)

1. 274
2. 8,342
3. 8,514
4. 72
5. square, 424
6. 7,722

Number Puzzle #2 (Page 33)

1. 47
2. 30
3. 13
4. 18
5. 14
6. 16
7. 12
8. 57
9. 76
10. 95

It All Adds Up #1 (Page 34)

6	2	5	9	1	8	4	3	7
1	4	7	5	2	3	8	6	9
8	9	3	7	4	6	1	5	2
7	3	8	4	9	1	5	2	6
4	6	2	3	8	5	9	7	1
9	5	1	2	6	7	3	4	8
3	1	6	8	5	2	7	9	4
5	8	4	6	7	9	2	1	3
2	7	9	1	3	4	6	8	5

It All Adds Up #2 (Page 35)

8	3	2	1	9	5	6	7	4
9	4	5	6	7	3	8	2	1
1	6	7	8	2	4	9	5	3
5	7	6	9	1	8	3	4	2
3	8	4	2	5	6	7	1	9
2	9	1	4	3	7	5	8	6
4	1	3	5	8	9	2	6	7
7	2	8	3	6	1	4	9	5
6	5	9	7	4	2	1	3	8

It All Adds Up #3 (Page 36)

6	4	8	7	5	1	2	9	3
2	9	1	6	3	4	5	8	7
5	7	3	8	9	2	4	6	1
4	2	7	1	6	5	9	3	8
3	1	6	9	4	8	7	5	2
9	8	5	2	7	3	1	4	6
7	5	4	3	2	6	8	1	9
1	6	9	4	8	7	3	2	5
8	3	2	5	1	9	6	7	4

It All Adds Up #4 (Page 37)

3	7	4	6	9	1	5	2	8
8	6	2	3	7	5	9	4	1
9	1	5	8	4	2	6	3	7
6	5	7	2	8	9	3	1	4
1	8	3	4	5	7	2	6	9
2	4	9	1	6	3	8	7	5
7	2	8	9	1	6	4	5	3
4	3	1	5	2	8	7	9	6
5	9	6	7	3	4	1	8	2

It All Adds Up #5 (Page 38)

7	9	2	3	5	8	1	6	4
1	8	6	7	4	9	5	3	2
5	4	3	2	1	6	7	9	8
8	7	4	9	6	2	3	5	1
2	3	5	4	7	1	6	8	9
6	1	9	8	3	5	4	2	7
9	5	7	6	2	4	8	1	3
3	6	8	1	9	7	2	4	5
4	2	1	5	8	3	9	7	6

It All Adds Up #6 (Page 39)

4	9	1	8	6	7	2	3	5
3	8	2	5	1	9	7	6	4
7	6	5	2	4	3	1	9	8
1	3	7	9	8	2	4	5	6
9	5	4	6	7	1	3	8	2
8	2	6	4	3	5	9	1	7
6	4	3	1	2	8	5	7	9
2	1	9	7	5	6	8	4	3
5	7	8	3	9	4	6	2	1

It All Adds Up #7 (Page 40)

3	9	2	8	4	5	6	1	7
6	7	5	2	3	1	9	8	4
8	4	1	6	7	9	5	3	2
7	1	4	5	6	8	3	2	9
9	3	6	4	2	7	8	5	1
5	2	8	9	1	3	7	4	6
1	5	7	3	9	2	4	6	8
4	8	9	1	5	6	2	7	3
2	6	3	7	8	4	1	9	5

It All Adds Up #8 (Page 41)

5	6	3	4	2	1	9	8	7
7	9	2	6	8	5	1	3	4
8	4	1	3	7	9	2	6	5
3	7	9	1	4	8	5	2	6
1	5	6	9	3	2	4	7	8
2	8	4	7	5	6	3	1	9
9	3	7	8	1	4	6	5	2
6	1	5	2	9	7	8	4	3
4	2	8	5	6	3	7	9	1

Get in Gear (Page 42)

1. $8,764 - 2,467 = 6,297$
2. $8,764 + 8,762 + 8,746 + 8,742 = 35,014$
3. $87,642 - 24,687 = 62,955$
4. $876 + 874 + 872 + 867 + 864 = 4,353$
5. $87,642 + 87,624 + 87,462 + 87,426 = 350,154$

Picking Apples (Page 43)

1. $98,763 - 36,789 = 61,974$
2. $987 + 986 + 983 + 978 + 976 = 4,910$
3. $987 \times 986 = 973,182$
4. $36 + 37 + 38 + 39 + 63 + 67 + 68 + 69 + 73 + 76 = 566$
5. $9,876 \times 36 = 355,536$

B-I-N-G-O! (Page 44)

Row Totals:

R1 = 203
R2 = 201
R3 = 159
R4 = 209
R5 = 187

Column Totals:

B = 57
I = 116
N = 158
G = 272
O = 356

Questions:

1. 299
2. 63
3. 50
4. 71

What's Missing? (Page 45)

1. Any 5-letter word that begins with "e" (e.g., eagle, elder, enjoy).
2. Any 4-letter boy's name that begins with "F" (e.g., Fred, Fran, Finn).
3. Any 4-letter word that begins with "j" and has double "e's" (e.g., jeep).
4. Any 4-letter word that begins with "n" (e.g., news, next, noon).
5. Any 5-letter word that begins with "l" (e.g., lambs, lease, loose).
6. Any country name that begins with "A" (e.g., Austria, Australia, Argentina).
7. Any 7-letter word that begins with "s" and ends with "er" (e.g., sticker, scatter, sharper).
8. Any 7-letter word that begins with "m" and ends with "e" (e.g., machine, manatee, massive).

Odd Word Out #1 (Page 46)

1. compassionate
2. minute
3. dreadful
4. factual
5. courageous
6. embark
7. mouth
8. Libya
9. avocado
10. crimson

Odd Word Out #2 (Page 47)

1. Dallas
2. murmur
3. ordinary
4. friend
5. Canada
6. daisy
7. Egypt
8. four
9. grief
10. herring

The Race Is Over (Page 48)

The winning car is #9706.

Puppy Predicament (Page 49)

Darby's ID Tag is #8975.

Cabin Chaos (Page 50)

The cabin number is #3329.

Who's Who? (Page 51)

Math—Stewart
English—Hanover
Geography—Mitchell
Science—Flagg
French—Gill
History—Eskell

State of Confusion (Page 52)

Sarah—Minnesota
Naomi—South Carolina
Allison—Kentucky
Kristin—New York
Veronica—Alabama
Margaret—Vermont

Birthday Month Mix-up (Page 53)

Jose—March
Mark—December
Fred—April
Derek—May
Max—February
Adam—January

Token Logic #1 (Page 54)

Token Logic #2 (Page 55)

Token Logic #3 (Page 56)

Phone Tag (Page 57)

Possible answers include:

1. cab, fed
2. jig, log
3. put, sty
4. high, pigs
5. back, bull
6. feed, deny
7. bait, moan
8. well, peel
9. bacon, tough
10. press, sleep
11. common, caught
12. sweeps, swells

Word$ Worth (Page 58)

Possible answers include:

1. part, trip
2. ware, bail
3. soft, door
4. done, hole

5. tile, pine
6. wrap, gait
7. poor, romp
8. west, best
9. stir, dirt
10. trap, part
11. rots, amid

Lucky Keystrokes (Page 59)

Possible answers include:

1. drab, helm
2. last, gasp
3. base, chat
4. pods, weds
5. bids, mild
6. blade, chase
7. blare, chart
8. wiped, worth
9. trace, react
10. threw, water
11. layer, skirt
12. ponds, tends

Put It All Together (Page 60)

Possible answers include:

1. spin, swing, brings
2. scan, spank, brands
3. hair, brain, drains
4. born, scorn, sports
5. bend, sends, wrench
6. heed, speed, creeks
7. pear, bread, preach
8. salt, chalk, stalks

File It (Page 61)

Possible answers include:

?ea? ➙ bean, leap, pear, tread
?oo? ➙ broom hoop, noose, stool
?ou? ➙ could, hour, mouse, tour
?ai? ➙ bait, gain, maize, trainer
?at? ➙ elate, hatred, matter, water
?or? ➙ corn, glorious, porter, vendors
?er? ➙ berry, heron, nerve, terrain
?st? ➙ beasts, jester, question, zesty

Color Pattern #1 (Page 62)

Yellow: 48, 80, 40, 8, 24, 15, 30

Light Blue: 130, 65, 52, 26, 91, 78, 117, 39

Green: 35, 98, 105, 112, 154

Red: 121, 81, 144, 100, 25

Light Purple: 17, 23, 47, 31, 53, 29, 19, 61

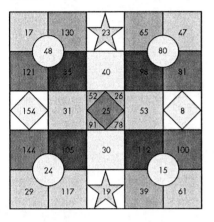

Color Pattern #2 (Page 63)

Yellow: friend, splash, tracked, branch

Light Blue: baggage, courage, transit, mirror

Light Green: cylinder, arachnid, carnivore, elephant, calendar

Pink: interior, elevator, alligator, tarantula, registration, photography, inventory, category

Light Purple: hippopotamus, electricity, educational, deforestation

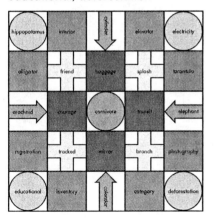

Satellite Radio (Pages 64–65)

Jazz—103
Hip-Hop—111
Latin—102
Rock 'n' Roll—107
Seasonal—100
Classical—104
Country—101
Bluegrass—108
Oldies—110
All Talk—106
Sports—109
News 24/7—105

Get in Shape (Pages 66–67)

1. 92
2. 37
3. 445
4. 7,917
5. 61
6. 266
7. 1,089
8. 16
9. 319
10. 110
11. 1,463
12. 1

What's for Lunch? (Pages 68–69)

Burger—12
Soup—1
Fruit—9
Salad—6
Spaghetti—4
Hot Dog—10
Ham & Cheese—5
Surprise—7
Taco—8
Chinese Food—2
Macaroni and Cheese—3
Pizza—11

Dazzling Design (Pages 70–71)

Row 1: yellow face, purple check mark Current Year, blue flower, red face

Row 2: orange sun, blue five-pointed star, red heart, yellow five-pointed star, black X

Row 3: red arrow pointing right, green triangle, purple diamond, green lightning bolt, yellow arrow pointing left

Row 4: green arrow pointing right, blue lightning bolt, black diamond, orange triangle, purple arrow pointing left

Row 5: black X, red five-pointed star, yellow heart, black five-pointed star, yellow sun

Row 6: blue face, green flower, initials, blue check mark, green face

Dazzling Design continued (Pages 70–71)

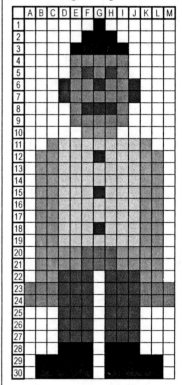

Robot Design (Page 72)

Draw a Police Pup (Page 73)

Drawing should look similar to picture in box 3 but with background details.

Draw a Motorcycle (Page 74)

Drawing should look similar to picture in box 4 but with background details.

Draw a Scene (Page 75)

Picture should look similar to the picture on the top of page.

Owl Portrait (Page 76)

Right half should look similar to the left half of page.

Draw an Ostrich (Page 77)

Right half should look similar to the left half of page.

Create a Clown (Page 78)

Right half should look similar to the left half of page.

Design an MP3 Player (Page 79)

Individual student drawings will vary.

Personal Banner (Page 80)

Individual student drawings will vary.

Design a CD Case (Page 81)

Individual student drawings will vary.

Create Comic Strips (Page 82–83)

Individual student drawings will vary.

Grid Picture #1 (Page 84)

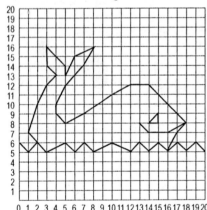

Grid Picture #2 (Page 85)

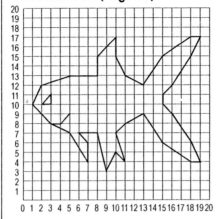

Grid Picture #3 (Page 86)

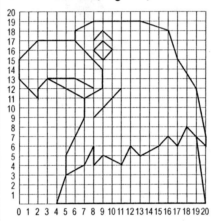

Win the Race (Page 87)

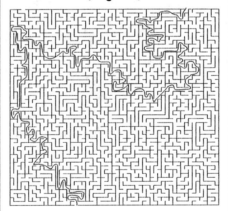

Sprint to the Finish Line (Page 88)

Catch a Butterfly (Page 89)

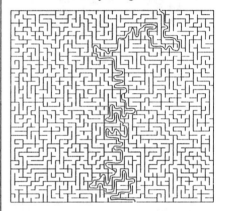

Find the Way Home (Page 90)

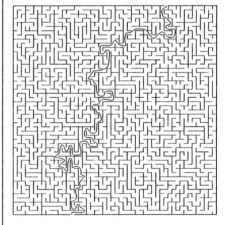